You Never Know

Selected Other Books by Ron Padgett

Great Balls of Fire

Toujours l'amour

Tulsa Kid

Triangles in the Afternoon

The Big Something

Blood Work: Selected Prose

Ted: A Personal Memoir of Ted Berrigan

New & Selected Poems

Albanian Diary

The Straight Line: Writings on Poetry and Poets

Poems I Guess I Wrote

Translations

The Poet Assassinated and Other Stories by Guillaume Apollinaire

Dialogues with Marcel Duchamp by Pierre Cabanne

Complete Poems by Blaise Cendrars

You Never Know

POEMS

BY RON PADGETT

COFFEE HOUSE PRESS

Minneapolis

Some of the poems in this book appeared in the following magazines: *Chicago Review, Columbia Poetry Review, Gare du Nord, Gas, The Harvard Advocate, The Hat, Michigan Quarterly Review, Milk, Shiny, Slate, Sulfur, Sycamore Review, Verse, Woodstock Journal,* and *The World.* Many thanks to the editors of these publications. One poem appeared as a Pressed Wafer broadside, courtesy of William Corbett. One appeared in a previous collection, *Poems I Guess I Wrote* (Cuz Editions), edited by Richard Hell. Others were included in four anthologies: *The Blind See Only This World: Poems for John Wieners* (Granary Books/Pressed Wafer), edited by William Corbett, Michael Gizzi, and Joseph Torra; *Best American Poetry 1993* (Collier Books), edited by Louise Glück; *Tributes: Celebrating Fifty Years of New York City Ballet* (Morrow), edited by Christopher Ramsey; and *Telling Stories: An Anthology for Writers* (Norton), edited by Joyce Carol Oates. "Feathers" and "Bang Goes the Literature" formed the texts of limited-edition collaborative books, beautifully designed and handmade by artist Bertrand Dorny. I also thank the staff of Coffee House Press, Allan Kornblum, Katy Beem, Anitra Budd, Christopher Fischbach, Josie Rawson, Linda Koutsky, and Molly Mikolowski, for their welcome, their enthusiasm, and their expertise. —R.P.

Coffee House Press is an independent nonprofit literary publisher supported in part by a grant provided by the Minnesota State Arts Board, through an appropriation by the Minnesota State Legislature, and in part by a grant from the National Endowment for the Arts. Significant support was received for this project through a grant from the National Endowment for the Arts, a federal agency. Support has also been provided by Athwin Foundation; the Bush Foundation; Buuck Family Foundation; Elmer L. & Eleanor J. Andersen Foundation; Honeywell Foundation; McKnight Foundation; Patrick and Aimee Butler Family Foundation; The St. Paul Companies Foundation, Inc.; the law firm of Schwegman, Lundberg, Woessner & Kluth, P.A.; Marshall Field's Project Imagine with support from the Target Foundation; Wells Fargo Foundation Minnesota; West Group; Woessner-Freeman family Foundation; and many individual donors. To you and our many readers across the country, we send our thanks for your continuing support.

Coffee House Press books are available to the trade through our primary distributor, Consortium Book Sales & Distribution, 1045 Westgate Drive, Saint Paul, MN 55114. For personal orders, catalogs, or other information, write to: Coffee House Press, 27 North Fourth Street, Suite 400, Minneapolis, MN 55401.

Library of Congress Cataloging-in-Publication Data

Padgett, Ron, 1942–
You never know : poems / by Ron Padgett.
p. cm.
ISBN 1-56689-128-0 (alk. paper)
I. Title.

PS3566.A32 Y68 2002
811'.54—DC21   2001052945

This book is for Pat.

Contents

Morning

Who is here with me?
My mother and an Indian man.
(I am writing this in the past.)
The Indian man is not a man,
but a wooden statue just outside
the limits of wood. My mother
is made of mother. She touches
the wood with her eyes and the eyes
of the statue turn to hers, that is,
become hers. (I am not dreaming.
I haven't even been born yet.)
There is a cloud in the sky.
My father is inside the cloud,
asleep. When he wakes up, he
will want coffee and a smoke.
My mother will set fire
to the Indian and from deep inside
her body I will tell her
to start the coffee, for even now
I hear my father's breathing change.

Glow

When I wake up earlier than you and you
are turned to face me, face
on the pillow and hair spread around,
I take a chance and stare at you,
amazed in love and afraid
that you might open your eyes and have
the daylights scared out of you.
But maybe with the daylights gone
you'd see how much my chest and head
implode for you, their voices trapped
inside like unborn children fearing
they will never see the light of day.
The opening in the wall now dimly glows
its rainy blue and gray. I tie my shoes
and go downstairs to put the coffee on.

To Myself

And another thing.
This same window
I looked out of
how many years ago
and heard my future
in the form of car tires
hissing against pavement
and now read of it
in a poem written that night
I had on an old bathrobe
black and gray and white
thick heavy cotton
out of a Thirties movie
and at the bottom
of which my legs stuck out
with wool socks on feet
that shuffled me over
to the window
that had raindrops
all over it and shuffled me
back to my desk to write
that poem, feeling moved
by the height of the quiet waiting,
an animal in the dark
wanting to sing in English.

Advice to Young Writers

One of the things I've repeated to writing
students is that they should write when they don't
feel like writing, just sit down and start,
and when it doesn't go very well, to press on then,
to get to that one thing you'd otherwise
never find. What I forgot to mention was
that this is just a writing technique, that
you could also be out mowing the lawn, where,
if you bring your mind to it, you'll also eventually
come to something unexpected ("The robin he
hunts and pecks"), or watching the "Farm News"
on which a large man is referring to the "Greater
Massachusetts area." It's alright, students, not
to write. Do whatever you want. As long as you find
that unexpected something, or even if you don't.

The Missing Lips

In the flower garden behind the cottage whose foundation rests in the gentle hills of Sussex, England, ca. 1920, a small black-and-white terrier is writhing around on the lawn and snorting in joy, snorting because he's had the urge to writhe and snort under the blue sunny sky, then trot off into the shade and plunk down on crossed paws and wait for Marian to come home from school, little Marian who feeds him treats and kisses him on what would be his lips if he had any!

Not Particularly

Out of the quarrel with life
we are a whirlwind
of invisible whirs that
go around a statue by Giacometti.
Or,
if putting new experiences
in a basket and taking them
on a picnic is the best way
to heal a wound, then
all of life is a way of forgetting
whatever it was.
There was something else besides a tree
at the end of the road, a train
waiting like a series of rulers
placed end to end, or like
the sensation of falling without information
and it is white,
or fairly white
and not particularly funny.

Fairy Tale

The little elf is dressed in a floppy cap
and he has a big rosy nose and flaring white eyebrows
with short legs and a jaunty step, though sometimes
he glides across an invisible pond with a bonfire glow on his cheeks:
it is northern Europe in the nineteenth century and people
are strolling around Copenhagen in the late afternoon,
mostly townspeople on their way somewhere,
perhaps to an early collation of smoked fish, rye bread, and cheese,
washed down with a dark beer: ha ha, I have eaten this excellent meal
and now I will smoke a little bit and sit back and stare down
at the golden gleam of my watch fob against the coarse dark wool of my vest,
and I will smile with a hideous contentment, because I am an evil man,
and tonight I will do something evil in this city!

Jay

The blue jay's cry goes up on stilts and takes
a few brisk strides through the mixed deciduous trees,
some of which rustle. It's not their answer.
They reach out and catch
him as he lands on branch and branch,
then flutters and stops: this
is his domain, and he is king.
He wears a little crown and in
his heart there is murder,
i.e., breakfast. The stilts rise again
in him and he cries out.

Sudden Flashes

hit the sky hot
as javelins vibrating in a baobab
that became a mast with chevrons
aflutter, and the ghost ship
floats into an icy abyss,
and the abyss heaves forth
a mighty guffaw shot through
with jagged rays of yellow light:
the curtain rises and before you
is a desert decorated with a solitary
snack bar owned and operated
by you! So get to work, you lout!
Serve up those corn dogs and *zut alors!*
the telephone. Another take-out order!

J & J

OK, here we go, running down the hill, the three of us, Jack
and Jill and you, the wind up, the clouds blowing left to right,
and Jill's hair bounding adorably, Jack's legs a little too short
for the rest of him, especially his head, big blond block head
and the deep chortle that issues from his red lips as he sees
Jill's sandal catch on a rock and her look of surprise as she
pitches forward into the haystack that you, the great artist,
were able to draw for her just in time.

For a Moment

It's funny how
if you just let go
of things they

will come to
you. That is to say
sometimes. So what

good is such a
generalization?
Ah, it makes you

feel good to say
such things from
time to time,

as if you actually
and really and truly
knew something!

Fixation

It's not that hard to climb up
on a cross and have nails driven
into your hands and feet.
Of course it would hurt, but
if your mind were strong enough
you wouldn't notice. You
would notice how much farther
you can see up here, how
there's even a breeze
that cools your leaking blood.
The hills with olive groves fold in
to other hills with roads and huts,
flocks of sheep on a distant rise.

My Son the Greek

I rather like the idea of having an adult
be my son,
            on top of a mountain turned
on its side and chained
to a flatbed truck
heading down a steep grade toward a cloud
called sleep.
All the little shepherds are snoozing, safe
and secure in the knowledge
that their sheep are facing forward
and not inside out. Yes,
it is good to bed down for the night
and the day and the intermission
in which you realize that you are alone
at the opera and the stage is empty
because the singing, the beautiful singing
and the very loud and beautiful singing is going
on inside your head that is now glued on
top of the neck of the boy whose birth made you cry out
to the hillsides on which the sheep were humming
as the stars listed to one side and went out.

Small Pond

As a child
I wanted to have a boat
and row
around a room
filled with money
the way
Scrooge McDuck
did, but I didn't
want to be
stingy or light
a cigar with
a twenty. I
just wanted to
see the coins
and bills fly
sparkling up
as oar and oar
went dipping
and churning.

Amsterdam

The sky has been scrubbed
by the sails in the harbor.
In the gutters of de Hooch
the rivulets are sparkling
because they are Dutch and
very clean. Even the bricks
are happy to be there, with
splashes of soapy water
on their faces every morning
and Benedict Spinoza inside
the house creating his book
theorem by theorem. Outside
the window a man says something
and a girl laughs and says, "No, Willem,
that is not the real reason."
Everything freezes.

What to Do

"Show, don't tell," they say, and I agree:
so here, take a look at my naked body, of which
I will tell you nothing, and here is my naked soul,
into which I will jump with both feet clad
only in socks, bright red ones from which
sparks are flying as I whiz into its depths.

Rectangle Obligation

I have a rectangle that I must fill. Overhead it resembles a rectangle, but seen from the side it is invisible, because it is an idea. I twang its sides and they vibrate, but so does everything else. A concert is coming up the road, and a whole sheet of laughter is ripping away from the surface and flying up the way this rectangle would if it had any energy. But it doesn't, until my head turns into wood and gets warm inside. Then the rectangle starts to glow and hum. Suddenly "hilarity bubbles" spread throughout the entire system and the four sides of the rectangle let go of each other and float off in different directions, rotating and tumbling slowly through the dark. I am very glad to be rid of it.

Embraceable You

I don't mind Walt Whitman's saying
"I contain multitudes," in fact I like it,
  but all I can imagine myself saying is
"I contain a sandwich and some coffee and a throb."
  Maybe I should throw my arms out and sing,
"Oh, grab hold of everything and hug tight!
  Then clouds, books, barometer, eyes wider
  and wider, come crashing through
  and leave me shattered on the floor,
  a mess of jolly jumping molecules!"

Obit Backlash

Today I read
in the *New York
Times* that
author James
Baldwin had
died of
cancer, in
France, at
his home,
and
I remembered
sitting in
an apartment
rental office
twenty-seven
years ago
and watching
the agent
ask an
applicant
if he was
a "friend"
of James
Baldwin, or
did he just
know him,
or had he
heard of

the apartment
through him
or any of
his friends,
and the guy
hesitated
and said
Well
yes sort of,
and the agent
said Get
out of this
office right
now! and turned
to me and said
Jesus Christ!
How may I
help you?

The Happy Whistler

When I was a child, the phrase "whistle while you work" came to mind easily not only because it was the title of a song made famous by the film *Snow White*, but also because people whistled. They whistled melodies while they worked, while they walked down the street, while they shaved. Men gave a wolf whistle when an attractive woman walked by, and they gave a loud whistle to get someone's attention, such as a taxi driver or fellow worker in the distance. Their mouths and tongues went into whistle positions, the breath was exhaled or inhaled, the eyes took on a casual inwardness, and the tones emerged into the air, sometimes pure and simple, sometimes with elaborate flourishes. When did widespread whistling begin to die out?

I taught myself to whistle, by trial and error, eventually becoming a passable whistler. In recent years, I have found myself walking down the street and whistling some tune or other that has been going through my head. Passersby glance at me and then look away. But I am immured inside the world of whistling. The mouth and tongue form various configurations, each one corresponding to a particular note, a note that my brain has miraculously chosen, but I don't know how I do it. My legs alternate in moving forward, thrilled with blood and sensation, but I don't understand how I control them. My heart is beating, my lungs are going up and down, my head turns to look left and right: I am like an aircraft carrier moving across the water with systems fully operational. A little man comes out and blows a whistle. Permission to come aboard?

The Austrian Maiden

I wish I had blonde hair
and was a maiden, on a farm, in Austria,

in the nineteenth century, on a sunny day,
with rosy cheeks and blue eyes, just

like those Nazi images of healthy farmgirls.
But are my great-grandchildren going

to be monsters? Then I will have none.
I will milk the cow and tell Hans

and the others to keep their mitts off me.
I will fill my evening hours with the sad music

of Schubert and the sad poetry of Heine.
It will be so beautiful.

Mountains Are a Feeling

Said Byron. I sat up
with a revision
of who he was because
of how he said that:
so straight out, and he
so windy and full
of commas. Mountains
are a feeling: the mountains
get inside him and he
in them, and then
he's free of Byron's body
and the rush to death.
I can see that, or thought
I could, as his four words
swept into me and I stayed
up until some other words
began to fly around inside
my head and out, and he
was gone again.

The County Fair

The Holstein looks at us with big eyes but with no expression in them. What images are flashing in its brain? The white goat walks over as if to ask a question, but it has no question to ask: there is no question mark in the goat world. The rabbit's pink eyes dilate when a hand draws near, but it does not move, and like a houseshoe, it says nothing. The two holes in the top of the goose's beak are in search of something to get huffy about: the poor goose is angry and without real nostrils. The black and white feathers exploding from the head of the rooster show that he is ready for war against the Infidel. The piglet walks and trots around with white eyebrows. He *likes* the Infidel.

The Abyss

We skid to a stop at the edge of what we realize is a cliff and our breath goes out over it and falls slowly into the abyss. The abyss is so hungry that it will accept even breath—it sends back a deep, hollow "thank you"—the abyss so empty of everything but sorrow. We put the car in neutral, get out, and shove it over the cliff. This time the abyss burps back its satisfaction. We empty our pockets, take off our clothes, and hurl everything over the edge. But we will not hurl ourselves. We will never do that, because nothing that falls into the abyss ever hits bottom.

The Saint Lurches

The trick is to have a feel
for which is the best way
to find the way to heaven
without using any idea of heaven
or any idea of anything: I
have an idea: the saint
says So What, My Child,
and sits down on a rock.
It is dry and empty
in the desert and it is
very dry and full inside
the rock that automatically
becomes the saint's heart,
thumping and banging. But
no one can hear them, this
sacred thumping and banging,
this silent lurching here
and there where no one is.

Voice and Fur

I touch my dog and she wags.
I straighten up the atmosphere
by viewing the fog and rain
through the screen door and she
takes a look too: dog eyes
that go flat gold and turn
to orbs. Her vocal mechanism
won't let her give out
the soft bursts of "papa" or
even the bubbles of baby talk.
So I talk to her so my voice can be
to her ear what her fur is
to my hand, drizzle across the clouds
that are now starting to separate.

Poem in a Manner Not My Own

To you, Max Jacob

It's Sunday, the day of rest. Should you lie back on a pink satin cushion and doze the afternoon away? But of course! This is, after all, 1889, and the boating party will not return for hours, and then you will hear the concertina from far away. You will have plenty of time to adjust your clothing and slick back your bushy eyebrows.

But wait, the boat has come back early, with no music! Skirts uplifted, the ladies are coming down the . . . you know, the slanting walkway down from the side of a ship that has docked, it has rope handrails, there is fog, and the foghorn gives out a foghorn blast, like the deep grunt of a whale that has eaten one of the ladies! The one with the concertina!

The Sweeper

I like to sweep the floor
with a cornstraw broom
and watch the dust mass up
and move along
each time I swing the broom.
I like the swoosh and scratch
along the boards
that brighten up as I go by.
And when I have a pile
that's big enough, I nudge it
in the dustpan, this way
and that, until it's all aboard,
except a thin line of dust
that can't be smaller.
Tough little dust! I raise
the broom up high and bring
it down and past the line
to make a gust and then
the tiny dust is gone. I love
my pan of big new dust.

Listening to Joe Read

I'm reminded that what made him great
was not that he was a great reader (he wasn't)
but that he was Joe: "History.
What with history piling up so fast,
almost every day is the anniversary
of something awful." Was Ted
in the audience at the Ear Inn
in 1983? I think I hear his chortle.
Joe's voice in my ear and his ashes
up in the meadow now dark, it's night.
I have plenty of time to say all this,
as long as Joe has time on this tape to read
as many times as I want to play it,
as if he's here, as of course he is,
inside this little brain,

its wheels turning round and round.

Bluebird

You can't expect
the milk to be delivered
to your house
by a bluebird
from the picture book
you looked at
at the age of four:
he's much older
now, can't carry those
bottles 'neath his wing,
can hardly even carry a tune
with his faded beak
that opens some nights
to leak out a cry
to the horrible god
that created him.

Don't think I'm
the bluebird, or that
you are. Let him get
old on his own and
die like a real bluebird
that sat on a branch
in a book, turned his head
toward you, and radiated.

Hug

The older I get, the more I like hugging. When I was little, the people hugging me were much larger. In their grasp I was a rag doll. In adolescence, my body was too tense to relax for a hug. Later, after the loss of virginity—which was anything but a loss—the extreme proximity of the other person, the smell of hair, the warmth of the skin, the sound of breathing in the dark—these were mysterious and delectable. This hug had two primary components: the anticipation of sex and the pleasure of intimacy, which itself is a combination of trust and affection. It was this latter combination that came to characterize the hugging I have experienced only in recent years, a hugging that knows no distinctions of gender or age. When this kind of hug is mutual, for a moment the world is perfect the way it is, and the tears we shed for it are perfect too. I guess it is an embrace.

Bobbie and Me on Bicycles

Reading Hazlitt's essay "On Going a Journey" tonight, I had the fleeting recollection of approaching a corner, in Holland. I was riding a bicycle down a quiet two-lane road, looking for the sign that would tell me where to turn right, onto the road to the museum. It was one of those days that seem pleasant in the memory because one can remember being neither hot nor cold. There must have been a sign, because I am making a right turn, and as I do I look back over my shoulder and see the face of my companion, which is smiling and sparkling, and which seems to be growing larger and larger as it detaches from her neck and floats up, tilted a little, like a balloon wafted by a breeze, and in the space around her head are pink and white ovals, slowly rotating and tumbling. By now we are pedaling straight down the road and her head has returned to normal, and the ovals have vanished. She is laughing a little, girlish and free, happy to be gliding along on a bicycle past the big trees on both sides of the road that is taking us to the museum.

And Oil

If a certain society of the past thought of you as a smelly, hairy beast who would eat tin cans, they might designate you as a scapegoat. But would a real goat care all that much? Surely the tin is brighter on the other side, the applause louder, because don't tin hands make more noise? The tin people are waiting for you with open arms.

Poem

Though we're all deep
it isn't that easy to be profound
and get away with it. Aeschylus
and Jimmy Schuyler do, though.
Jimmy's flowers plunge into a more resonant
version of themselves while staying
exactly the same. How do they do that?
The surface of this table
is a smooth white that starts to suggest
something else and then doesn't. It's
just a tabletop. When I run my fingers
over it, it makes a cool swoosh.
I do it again. Cool swoosh.

The Drummer Boy

Oh what a sleepy night! The eyelids are drooping, the shoulders are slumped, the nostrils are wheezing, and Tommy the miniature drummer boy statue is yawning in the haystack where he landed last night when the farmboy hurled him into the dark sky. And now above the new-mown fields the stars burst into the drummer boy's brain and rain silver fear into his nervous system. He will have to get used to the fact that—oh, it makes me tired just to think of it—the fact that there are so many miles between him and the stars that are so immense but look so small and may not even be there anymore, just as he is not there anymore for the farmboy, the boy who himself will soon be leaving home.

Medieval Salad Dive

I don't see why I can't dive into that salad bowl
and rough up the lettuce, shaking my blubbery jowls
and uttering great guttural growls, Grrr, I'm
a medieval German and I'm feeling frisky and
in need of salad dressing! So bring on the fine lady
who wails perpetually, "O Wotan, strike me dead
if I'm to face another day!" Strike the tambour
and stomp your cruddy feet, men of my tribe,
for tonight I dive into the salad bowl!

The Drink

I am always interested in the people in films who have just had a drink thrown in their faces. Sometimes they react with uncontrollable rage, but sometimes—my favorites—they do not change their expressions at all. Instead they raise a handkerchief or napkin and calmly dab at the offending liquid, as the hurler jumps to her feet and storms away. The other people at the table are understandably uncomfortable. A woman leans over and places her hand on the sleeve of the man's jacket and says, "David, you know she didn't mean it." David answers, "Yes," but in an ambiguous tone—the perfect adult response. But now the orchestra has resumed its amiable and lively dance music, and the room is set in motion as before. Out in the parking lot, however, Elizabeth is setting fire to David's car. Yes, this is a contemporary film.

You Never Know

1) What might happen.
2) How people will behave.
3) Oh anything.

Three rules that live
in the house next door.

Along comes the big bad philosopher,
and at their door
he hurls the mighty bolts
of lightning
from his brain.

The door is unimpressed.
Behind it the rules
are chuckling.

I witness this scene
through the kitchen curtains
as I rinse the dishes.

A Prescription for a Happy Sort of Melancholy

A small gray-brown bird sat on the power line and chirped a few times, flipping its tail up and down. Then it flew a few feet over to a branch, where it sat, jerking its head this way and that. Then it flew off into the heavier woods, but a moment later returned, landing on a higher branch, then flapped up to an even higher one. After looking around and chirping a few more times, it fell silent, flicking its tail. It seems contented, perhaps because it is plump and alert, prosperous and chipper. The branches cannot complain about the bird's landing on them: they are deeply involved in branchness, so deeply they do not even "know" the bird is there. The bird doesn't know I'm watching. What is watching me? I am watching me.

Metaphor of the Morning

The morning is as clean and bright
as a freshly shaved cheek splashed with water
and rubbed with a new white towel.
Ah, the joys of metaphor!

But what if the morning were as dirty as
an old hag with a wen for a head
that is licking its chops and drooling on you?
Ah, the joys of metaphor!

But what if a blank metaphor descended from the sky
and landed lightly in your living room,
a cloudy, shifting swirl of gray tones and smoke?
It would be a Greek god! It would scare you!

Toybox

Let's say that we have only one number, one shape, and one color: six, square, and dun. No, let's not say that. Let's have two numbers, one shape, and three colors: two and two, a triangle, red, white, and green. Wait, isn't two and two just one number? No. You are a man with two triangular heads. Your face is green, with red eyes and teeth and white hair and nostrils. Your nostrils are sneeze exits. Achoo! Achoo! Two and two triangles of sneeze zoom out and fade, like fireworks in the night sky, glittering and falling to the *oooh*s and *aaah*s of your red lips, your wooden lips that we must now put back in the box, which we close and slide back under the bed.

To Anne Porter

I never wrote back to you about
the poem you sent at Christmas
because I did not know how to, exactly.
The shouting voices in the dark
hills a few days A.D.
brought out a scary memory in my head
of actually being there, one of those
shepherds, the one who felt suddenly tender
and filled with exploding ladders of light
whose sparks fell among the sleepy animals.
I wanted to come back swiftly
to tell you I'm still there
for you, though not for me myself.
The me myself floats up the evening street from work
a wisp of muscled doubt
invisible in the snow falling among traffic lights.

The Future of Your Name

Put the word *Marvin*
in front of any other word
and you'll see it's funny.
But if you put it
after any word, it isn't.
If you say only the first
syllable, pause, and say
the second, it will lose
all meaning, just as some day
your name will lose all meaning.
Its phonemes will dash about
in search of meaning, but
the future won't have any meaning
left for it. It will be all used up.

A Rude Mechanical

Whisk the curtain away and reveal
the new scene, hurrah!
it's the little village
again, with its little villagers
and the light coming
from everywhere
on this day without sun.
Their blue faces fly
around in the air
and red and green stripes
crisscross the atmosphere,
for today is a holiday
and the cows are folded up
and placed inside of envelopes
in the cool barns. But now
I must think of something
to say in my speech. "My dear
fellow villagers. . . ." Yes,
that's the stuff!

Poet as Immortal Bird

A second ago my heart thump went
and I thought, "This would be a bad time
to have a heart attack and die, in the
middle of a poem," then took comfort
in the idea that no one I have ever heard
of has ever died in the middle of writing
a poem, just as birds never die in mid-flight.
I think.

The Idea of Rotterdam

This idea
has an undertow like a philosopher
staring at breakfast in a room
whose dim light comes in through one small window
and his wife is clanging pots and pans
as in a comic strip, and all of Rotterdam goes
out and hits the windowsills with hot
soapy water like those big puffy clouds
tinged with gray and pushed across the sky
above the lowing cattle whose shepherd boy
now turns to look at you
and then away, his hat flapping
in the wind this
way and that.

Exceptions to the Rule

I take exception to the rule
that says I may not love you forever
because that's too long a time
for mortal man: we get forever
minus a big chunk.
More than a bug gets.
Such as the one I just killed.
A watched pot never boils
unless you watch it after it boils,
and then all the water is gone,
up in smoke, like spirit,
for the spirit is thoroughly exceptional,
subject to its own regulations:
everything is one-time only,
like the glass electric gun of Alessandro Volta,
like the formation of these words in their ink drying,
subject to smudge. I lean
to kiss you: we are smudged
by each other's softness
and a little of it rubs off on us,
like the smile as it first entered
the environment several hundred thousand years ago
via the exceptional head of homo sapiens
who still unrolls a red carpet
in your idea of yourself: out there
a fresh breeze is rising about the faces
of young girls still so pretty and free,
the way I want to be
the originator of a chain reaction
that sends a jagged love throughout the world and on.

Crossing the Alps

Are you really going to try? That's a pretty steep drop. I wouldn't even get close to the edge if I were you. It has a grassy fringe that looks friendly, but remember, this is a drawing in a style that is meant to look friendly. Even that stone on the left looks as though it had been put there just to say howdy. But don't be deceived: because the line of the cliff extends no further than the bottom of the paper, you have no way of knowing how far down it goes. And the echo you hear is simply the memory of the sound of a word you thought of saying, but didn't. So if you want to get to the other side, I wouldn't just run and leap. I'd get another piece of paper and draw a nice, sturdy bridge, over which some clouds are floating. This one drawing is not enough.

Think and Do

I always have to be doing something, accomplishing something, fixing something, going somewhere, feeling purposeful, useful, competent—even coughing, as I just did, gives me the satisfaction of having "just cleared something up." The phone bill arrives and minutes later I've written the check. The world starts to go to war and I shout, "Hey, wait a second, let's think about this!" and they lay down their arms and ruminate. Now they are frozen in postures of thought, like Rodin's statue, the one outside Philosophy Hall at Columbia. His accomplishments are muscular. How could a guy with such big muscles be thinking so much? It gives you the idea that he's worked all his life to get those muscles, and now he has no use for them. It makes him pensive, sober, even depressed sometimes, and because his range of motion is nil, he cannot leap down from the pedestal and attend classes in Philosophy Hall. I am so lucky to be elastic! I am so happy to be able to think of the word *elastic*, and have it snap me back to underwear, which reminds me: I have to do the laundry soon.

My Trip to Italy

And the white silk blossomed and bloomed and blew over the
        white bed out into the room in the hill town that flew
        each night over all of Italy to see that all was well and
        it was,
And it was wonderful, actually, in place, straight up and down,
        with curves, and ideas, such as where is my old friend
        now, my old friend who now is never aging here or
        there, as in *ecco mi qua,* and out I go into the sunlight,
        as a star goes out into space and becomes a stove,
        bing! tac!
And those rays of light you see everywhere, that traveling stig-
        mata that sets fire to a little patch of forehead, oh! ouch!
        hey! I don't want to be a saint, get off my forehead,
Because I have a red fire engine and a red fire of my own, two
        yellow dogs go woof, one in each of my ears as I enter
        and the walls slide to and fro a little, I get scared, I'll
        never take an airplane again!
Except I do, one whose curtains are decorated with a cherry
        motif and a border of little blue ducks because this is a
        children's airplane drifting o'er the clouds besmashed
        with radiant gold streaks across the stratosphere and,
        ah, the service, the in-flight rumba and the rum punch,
        knocked silly, sideways, big tears in your eyes.

Haiku

That was fast.
I mean life.

The Periscope

"I"
    is the way to see things as if
    through a periscope
    through which fear arrives
    or the satisfaction of the captain
    and the crew when the enemy explodes.
    And then we dive, dive
    and hide deep down, go
    inside ourselves like animals
    whose memories have lost the things
    they've killed as well as who they are,
    a great gift and greater terror
    when animal and angel unite behind a star
    the skinny "I" floats past in the dark.

Little Ode to Suzanne Farrell

No ode is big
        or fast enough to have
the very all of you inside it
        so I will have to be like you
and climb inside myself and fly
            into the outline that the pattern
of my moving self has left behind

the outline of the possible you impossibly beautiful in everyone

like a little girl suddenly seeing the angles in
a light blue protractor and therefore being them

Where was I and who?

You for whom
we get dressed up
and go uptown and up
the elevator shaft as
    the curtain goes up and when
        you glide in on your diagonal
we fall into the elevation of the dream
    that has a hummingbird and Saint Teresa of Avila in it

            and you

who hover in the air like a disembodied heart
shocked into eternity for the split second the music

turns to face you and you find your face up there
in the dark where we are and a smile on it

There is space here and air and breath, clarity
    of perfect tears that beauty makes us cry so automatically

        as you wrap the world around
    your finger, then wrap yourself
                around the world

Bob Creeley Breakthrough

This is going well today
I mean the fingers typing
and the face smiling
and the breath going in and out

like a nice girl on a date
who for the first time removes
her blouse, but your heart

is pounding so hard you
can't actually
see anything
except a mental
image
of Robert
Creeley

—Bob, go away
so I can see this girl and do
whatever it is I'm supposed to
do. Your linebreaks
are making it
impossible!

How to Become
a Tree in Sweden

I look up ahead and see
the trees of Sweden waving at me

Gently they wave their bending heads
The light goes dim above the land

And down below the lights come on
And Swedish people one by one

Come out to shop and say hello
as crisply as a Swedish cracker that

fresh out of the package goes snap.
And soon the air is full of snaps

And schnapps and weimaraners and
me, my various selves united,

for a moment Swedish, a tree myself,
waving and lost among the others.

Aquamarine Fantasy

Me? I am presently falling off the front end of a great battle-ship, to honor the god of the sea, Frank O'Hara. We are little figurines in a bottle you can see through and can't figure out how we got in there. Heigh ho! Wooden waves advance against our noses, but to no avail, for Frank and I, with the wind in our spirits, sail bravely on. Heigh ho! Our bottle rolls away. Heigh ho! The highballs are jiggling their ice cubes and the tropical images are swirling amidst the frosted panes, the fish are hanging in mid-air outside. They form a pattern that continues onto the seashore and the hills, onto the department store and your pajamas, onto the aria and the idea. Drink hearty, lads, for tonight we're falling off the front end of a great battleship, the *Frank O'Hara*.

Frisky

The black-and-white terrier
flexed his body
in mid-air, turned
and yelped

It was his birthday
and he was two

Elegy

It's a little too dark and deep the ocean
for me. It's a little too "offset press."
And if gorilla, striped rubber ball, and baby
disappear, there's always the way they
disappeared, to think about, and find inside,
and take it outside, and place it on the ground,
and sing the light up out of it, whoosh, into
the clouds, to make you happy, and not fall down,
and dinner is on time and where it should be,
on the table, this evening, again!

Feathers

fly up and pow apart
from the bird they were.

Now we will shoot the post
and kill the fence. It is

good to knock things down
and destroy them. We are

like a good storm or an
earthquake and some lava.

Life will come back by itself.
And we will come back too.

We are not bad people.
We are happy monsters.

Flash Photo

Once again I am having the fantasy of seeing my father on the front porch at night as he watches the rain come down through the trees, but this time, instead of standing behind him, I am hurled around and I see his face, his actual face with light on it, and his eyes open, and it is so real and frozen in time that I cannot bear to look. I jump up from my chair and walk around.

Old Song

What kind of fool am I?
An older fool!
The bells on my costume
gleam dully
in the flickering firelight.
A moth flutters
around my cap.
The massive King snores massively
in his massive chair.
Dare I wake him?
Or tiptoe down the hall?
An ember crumbles.
Would that I,
like the humble bee,
were flying back to paradise!

The Poet's Breakfast

What does a writer do? A writer sits and goes through hell.
I'm not exactly going through hell, but then, I'm not driven by
the belief that the world is waiting for my next bit of hard-
earned genius. No, I would rather be raking and piling the
grass, wrapping the two weeping birches for the winter, or
patching the hole in the wood stove. I seem to feel that since I
can do nothing to save souls, it is my job to slow the material
world's inevitable slide into rack and ruin. I like the material
world. I think objects should be respected, the same as people
and ideas. I even respect art, especially when we consume it
and it becomes us. Juan Gris's 1914 painting *Breakfast* became
part me in 1962, when I first saw it. I had never seen anything
that was beautiful in the way that it was beautiful. I should add
that I was looking at it with Joe Brainard, who knew how truly
beautiful it was, and I was seeing it through his eyes and want-
ing to leap into the paint and be refracted through and along
its various angles and disappearances. And now, as Joe and I
drive to town, I'm struck by how bizarre it is that in a few
years he will be gone and by how brave he is to keep enjoying
the details of everyday life. I am forty-nine years old and sur-
rounded by death. Does writing help? Probably not.

I Guess

I had forgotten that
when Ted Berrigan sent
Conrad Aiken his *Sonnets*
Aiken rebuked him, and
the letter was published
in *The Collected Letters*
of Conrad Aiken—one
of his last, actually—
so that when I
read about it yesterday
in an interview Ted
gave, I was surprised:
the blue fox jumped
over the black log
and ran like hell.

Lullaby

Another little poem
before I go to bed
and there to sleep,
a little poem to bid
the world goodnight
and lay me down to sleep
inside the warmth
of being fast asleep,
then slow and slower,
down into the deep
warm way we have
of sinking to the far away
inside our body's self,
inside our pillow head,
inside our sleeping bed.

The Song of Grandpa

Let's take the squeak of a chair.
Not creak. Creak is for wood. This
is a squeaking spring, a sound effect
for when grandpa stands up: *squeak,*
Oh no, it's his stiff back! Grandpa puts
a hand back there and groans a little.
He does this every time, even when
his back has been removed by thought,
such as the one that has him in Egypt
with a scepter and tall hat, and the light
is flickering across his face as he breaks out
in eery, holy song and the Pharaoh himself
kneels down and weeps. The high priest
wails out his melody, and Egypt weeps.

Music

He was listening to the lariat as its loop swept round and round above his head and he stood perfectly still, hat and chaps unmoving, eyes fixed on the ground, which had only some dust and the marks to show where his feet should go at various points in the performance. It looked like a diagram for the tango, only it was in full color and tilted slightly toward him, as if to make it easier to read. But nothing could be made easier for the cowboy whose tears were ready to burst forth, nothing could be made easier for him.

Wisconsin

It's hard to find that little room again,
the one you like to find yourself in
but not have to find. A certain plateau of tranquility
spreads evenly over the face of the coming night
and there is large smiling in the cracked darkness.
The puzzle holds, though, even when your little sister
tips the table over with a silent crash
against the loud floor. And now there is some
two-colored radiation from the carolers
who have upper bodies and lower stilts
that vault their voices into a Renaissance
whose inside is entirely covered with a floral pattern
and cisterns placed every twenty steps along
the long hallway that leads to the little room
with its fireplace and burning logs
and terrible buildup of soot on the stone legs
of the Fireplace Giant, who seems born
for this terrible destiny, always to have
darkened legs and flaring eyebrows
that rise as if lifted by invisible threads
into the evening above his stocking cap,
a blue dome that holds in his massive idea
that thunders in the distance and wants out.

Bang Goes the Literature

Bang! goes the gun. Big bang! goes the shotgun.
Bong! says the shogun.
The sound waves of his bong emanate out into the clear night
that is taking place in what
the French call *le Japon, avec son soir japonais.*
Pan! dit the fusil. *Pain!* dit le shogun, *pain
pour tout le monde.* Il prend son fusil et tire
sur les baguettes qui volent dans le soir japonais.
And all the rest is literature.

The Lips of the Dairymen

It's midnight, and the thirteen dairymen are working at fever pitch, in a desperate effort to save their company, the little creamery in the hills. And they are singing a song from the old country, a plaintive song about being slaughtered by Cossacks, but rather than depressing them it seems to feed an inner glow that radiates out through their dark blue lips. Along the rounded sides of the silver vats, the reflections of their lips curve, glint, and slide away.

Morning Poem

Open the side window and let
the morning air in and the light
that has erased the fog
so chirping comes in
as if to say "It's alright, Ron,
we're here just as
we've always been,
the same blue jay on Fourth Street
in 1952 as now," the robin
redbreast, the wrens and sparrows
and all those others inside my chest
when they call out to say
"This is my place, my cage."

Album

The mental pictures I have of my parents and grandparents and my childhood are beginning to break up into small fragments and get blown away from me into empty space, and the same wind is sucking me toward it ever so gently, so gently as not even to raise a hair on my head (though the truth is that there are very few of them to be raised). I'm starting to take the idea of death as the end of life somewhat harder than before. I used to wonder why people seemed to think that life is tragic or sad. Isn't it also comic and funny? And beyond all that, isn't it amazing and marvelous? Yes, but only if you have it. And I am starting not to have it. The pictures are disintegrating, as if their molecules were saying, "I've had enough," ready to go somewhere else and form a new configuration. They betray us, those molecules, we who have loved them. They treat us like dirt.

The Love Cook

Let me cook you some dinner.
Sit down and take off your shoes
and socks and in fact the rest
of your clothes, have a daquiri,
turn on some music and dance
around the house, inside and out,
it's night and the neighbors
are sleeping, those dolts, and
the stars are shining bright,
and I've got the burners lit
for you, you hungry thing.

Nuts

I read *Fear and Trembling*
expecting to be scared
but instead I found a nut
had written it in Denmark,
a man obsessed with thoughts
about the story of Abraham and Isaac
and what it meant. I didn't see
what it had to do with fear *or*
trembling, but the more I read
the more I liked the title and
its being on that book. I guess
I am a nut too.

When George Calls

I'm looking forward to the moment when George calls me from Italy to say that he's just gotten a phone installed. It is always a pleasure to talk to George when he's across the ocean, but it will be an even greater pleasure that he will be using his own phone to call me at my own phone. We will be two grown-up men talking on our own phones from our own homes. Why does that thought give me such pleasure?

And Was It Leeds?

For Trevor Winkfield

At an early age I should have started writing books for children. Well, I did, but they weren't suitable for children. And they weren't really books. They were whiffs of books. A few adults liked the whiffs, but I could see that these adults were strange. That is, they were artists, tiny artists only a foot or so tall, barely able to lift the books they read, hearts going thump thump thump.

People with Heads

I am unafraid of the guillotine
because they would never chop off the head
of a stick figure, the shape
I assume when I travel back
into the past far enough
that you never can tell what the locals
might do to you. I stand
in the Place de la Concorde and watch
the rising, heavy blade and I gleam.
These poor fools! They
chop and chop, head after head,
but no matter how fast they chop,
there are always more and more
people with heads.

Pensée juste

Gustave Flaubert—how did his breath
smell as he roared out each phrase
alone in his room, night after night?
Bad, I bet, the drooping mustache hairs
blown out by the booming wind,
Mom's cutlery rattling in the sideboard,
the dog trembling beneath the cupboard, and
Mom herself turning down the gaslight
and slipping into bed with the thought,
"He's perfectly normal."

Ape Man

Why is it that I seem to want to write so often about writing? I'm not a theoretician of language. I do seem to feel, though, that there is something about writing that no one has ever quite described or explained, something about the way words are like a food chain that goes down simultaneously to the smallest creature and to the pit of our stomachs. But that doesn't come near to the mystery. Perhaps it can't be put into words, because words can't be used to describe themselves, just as an eye can't see itself. It can see only a reflection of itself, a glimpse at the fascination of being, like the pre-human creature that got split in half by the shimmering water he was about to drink. He bent down and drank from his own lips. I bend down and suck my own words up off the page.

The Woodpecker Today

The wings of the red-headed woodpecker flashed white as he landed on the deck rail, well fed and magisterial, and rattled off a quick succession of pecks. Then he hopped and drilled again, paused and drilled, then raised his head and turned his neck to the left, as if to receive a message from the sky. Then he sprang into the air and flew around the side of the house. There were two brief bursts of drilling, then silence.

While he was drilling the rail, I recalled an article that explained why woodpeckers don't get headaches. Apparently their skulls are lined with a spongy material that cushions the shock, a structure that resembles that of a football helmet. In fact, the article stated, modern football helmet design owes something to the woodpecker. As these thoughts ran through my head, for a moment I saw a small helmet materialize on the woodpecker's head—a silver Detroit Lions helmet. I hope he comes back. I would like to get the entire uniform on him.

Little Elegy

Blaise Cendrars in his final days, old
and ill, wrote down his final words:
This morning on the windowsill a bird.
I find that so beautiful and moving
I can barely stand it, though
it makes me see the aged poet, head
turned toward the window and a small bird
perched there, staring in, angling its head
at the bulbous nose and squinty eyes:
I have come to visit you, old man.
But now I'll lift my wings and they will beat,
for flying is my great thrill,
and where the wings sprout out
is calling me to leap and fly.
Good-bye.
Morning, windowsill, and bird
all flown away. Good-bye, good-bye.

Sacred Heart

Last night I dreamed that my sister-in-law and I were snugly bedded in a dark cocoon, talking softly, safe and alone. With that part of me that once was in love with her, I said, "I missed you when you were gone."

"Oh," she said, "you missed me because I speak English."

"No, I really just missed *you.*"

It was deeply satisfying to open my heart this way.

My father had torn off his oxygen mask, flung his gown onto the floor, and now, stark naked and peeing into the air, was clambering, tubes and all, over the bed railing, giving loud grunts.

I sprang up, grabbed him by the shoulders, and slowly talked him back down onto his pillow, where he drifted off again. After mopping the floor, I went back to my cot.

It was still dark out.

I lay down and thought about my dream, the dream that was filled with the same rush of sweetness that had come over me the day before, when I had looked out the hospital window, at early light, and far below saw a person walking down the street alone, and felt the words *thank you* bursting from my chest.

Amy,

it's interesting that
no matter how one starts
a poem, the poem can lead
to something else.
I left home
to grow into
the poet I thought
I'd like to be, the one
whose work would
show the way he found
to live at peace with
his mortality. So
far I've only found the way
to go upstairs
and bang against the wall
of silence, the one that moves
from room to room,
and laugh. It's fun
to stand there
puzzled for a wink,
then go back down
and ping! remember
what I went up for
and go back up
for it. And there
it is: this poem for you.